Jyoti R. McMinn

3.98

7205 Illinois, LR, Ak. 72207

Baking

Baking

GALLERY BOOKS

An Imprint of W. H. Smith Publishers Inc.

112 Madison Avenue

New York City 10016

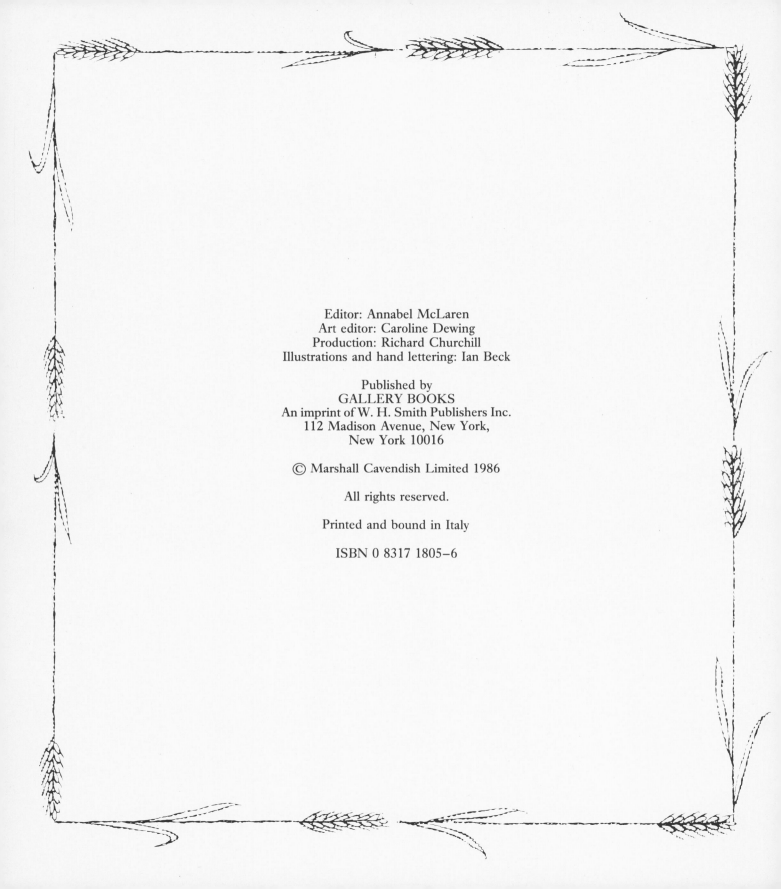

Editor: Annabel McLaren
Art editor: Caroline Dewing
Production: Richard Churchill
Illustrations and hand lettering: Ian Beck

Published by
GALLERY BOOKS
An imprint of W. H. Smith Publishers Inc.
112 Madison Avenue, New York,
New York 10016

Printed and bound in Italy

ISBN 0 8317 1805−6

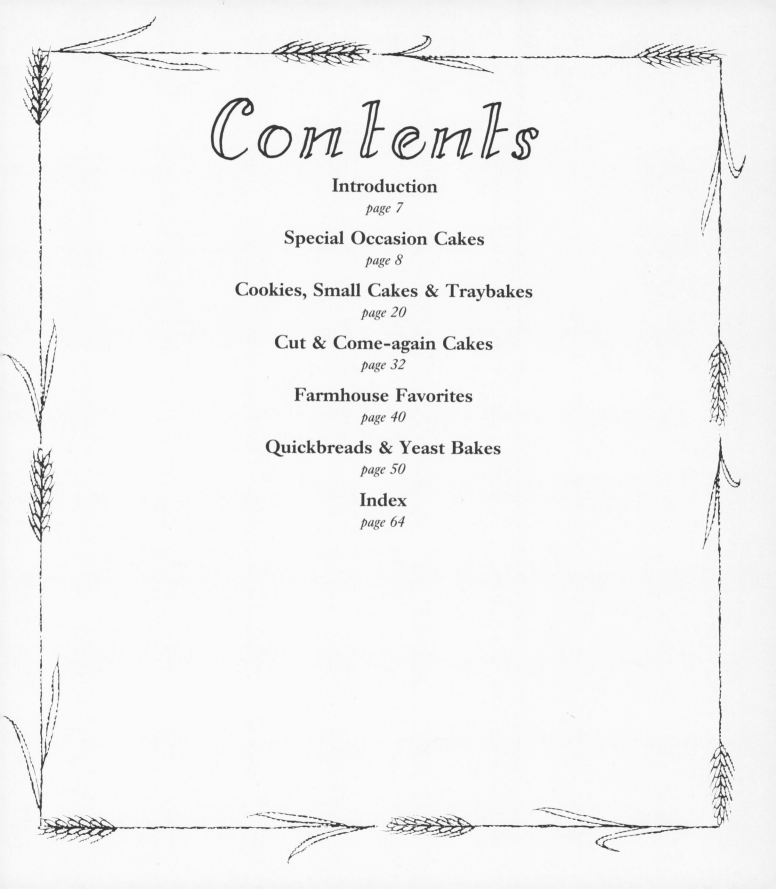

Contents

Introduction

Nothing conjures up the image of the country kitchen more effectively than the aroma of baking – freshly baked breads, cookies and cakes, full of natural ingredients, are a sure reminder of the wholesome fare to be found down on the farm. With Country Kitchen Baking you have the chance to bring the aromas of the country into your own kitchen – the cakes, cookies and bread recipes featured here are sure to tempt you into rolling up your sleeves and kneading dough!

For ease of reference the recipes are divided into five parts: Special Occasion Cakes; Cookies, Small Cakes and Traybakes; Cut and Come Again Cakes; Farmhouse Favorites; Quickbreads and Yeast Bakes. Some of the cookies and cakes are simple to make, others are more complicated – whatever the cake, many are sure to become firm favorites, made time and time again.

From simple Irish soda bread and drop biscuits cooked on the griddle to delicious Florentines, Madeleines and Macaroons, Country Kitchen Baking gives you a cookie, cake or bread for every day of the week. And not only are there such traditional standbys as Dundee cake and Pound cake, there are also mouth-watering cakes for special occasions – from a christening or an anniversary to a family birthday. Whatever the event you are celebrating, the special-occasion cake you choose is certain to honor the occasion in style – and have your guests coming back for more!

Special Occasion Cakes

Special occasions call for special cakes, and in this chapter we give you a mouth-watering selection to choose from – delicious sponge cakes, melt-in-the-mouth fudge cakes, an impressive Battenburg, jelly roll variations and a cheesy-topped carrot cake. Whether you are planning a family celebration – a birthday, a Christening or an anniversary, for example – or simply making a cake for somebody special, you are sure to find the perfect recipe here. And just because these cakes are a little out of the ordinary does not mean that they are all complicated to make – while some are, others are quite easy. These cakes – straight from the country kitchen – are sure to be a success!

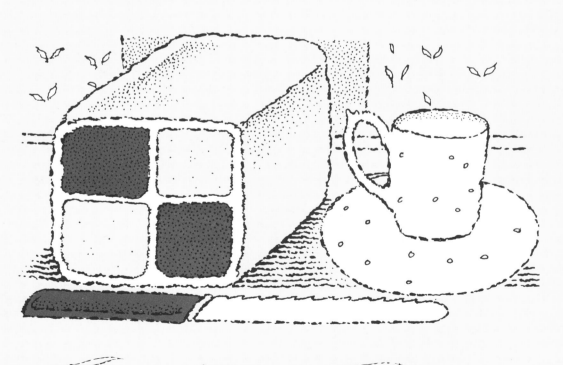

Battenburg cake

Makes 6 slices

½ cup soft butter or margarine
½ cup superfine sugar
2 eggs, lightly beaten
1 teaspoon vanilla
1 cup self-rising flour, sifted
few drops of red food coloring
pan spray, for greasing
TO FINISH
5 tablespoons apricot jam
1 package (7 oz) marzipan
superfine sugar, for sprinkling

1 Preheat the oven to 375°F. Grease a loose-bottomed 8 inch square cake pan, line the base with waxed paper, then grease the paper.

2 Cut a rectangle of foil 16 × 12 inches. Fold across twice to make a strip 12 × 4 inches.

3 Place the foil strip across the center of the pan (to divide it in half) and fold both ends flush with the side of the pan. Secure the ends with paper clips, then grease the foil with pan spray.

4 Beat the butter and superfine sugar until pale and fluffy. Add the eggs, a little at a time, beating thoroughly after each addition, then beat in the vanilla. Using a metal spoon, fold in the flour.

5 Spoon half the batter into one-half of the prepared pan and level the surface. Tint the remaining batter pink with food coloring, then spoon into the other half and level the surface.

6 Bake just above the center of the oven for about 30 minutes, until the cakes are golden and springy to the touch. Leave them in the pan to cool.

7 Remove the paper clips. Carefully remove the side of the pan. Slide a spatula knife under each cake to loosen it from the lining paper, then separate the cakes by easing them away from the foil.

8 Trim the cakes exactly the same size and cut each in half lengthwise.

9 Strain the jam into a small saucepan and stir over low heat until melted. Using some of the jam, stick one pink and one white strip together, side by side. Then stick the remaining strips on the top, reversing the colors.

10 Knead the marzipan until smooth. Sprinkle the working surface generously with superfine sugar, then roll out the marzipan to a rectangle, the same length as the cake and about 2½ times its width. Brush the top of the cake with jam, then wrap it in the marzipan, sealing the seam firmly.

11 Place the cake, seam side down, on a serving platter. Mark a diamond pattern on the top of the cake and sprinkle superfine sugar over.

Coffee gateau

Makes 12 slices

2 cups self-rising flour
1 teaspoon baking powder
1 cup soft margarine
1 cup superfine sugar
4 large eggs, beaten
1 tablespoon cold strong black coffee
melted margarine, for greasing
FILLING
⅓ cup soft butter
2 packages (3 oz size) cream cheese
2½ cups confectioners' sugar, sifted
2 teaspoons cold strong black coffee
⅔ cup chopped walnuts
14 walnut halves, for decoration

1 Preheat the oven to 350°F and grease two 8 inch layer cake pans. Place a round of waxed paper in the base of each, then grease them.

2 Sift the flour and baking powder into a large bowl. Add the soft margarine, superfine sugar, eggs and coffee and beat vigorously for 2–3 minutes until smoothly blended.

3 Divide the cake batter equally between the 2 prepared pans, smoothing the surface so that the batter is level.

4 Bake in the oven for 25–30 minutes until just firm to the touch. Let the cakes stand in the pans for a few minutes, then invert on a wire rack. Peel off the lining paper and let cool.

5 To make the filling: Beat the butter and cheese together until light and fluffy. Beat in the confectioners' sugar, 1 tablespoon at a time until half has been incorporated, then beat in the coffee before adding the remaining sugar. Beat ½ cup chopped nuts into one-third of the buttercream.

6 When cold, assemble the gateau: Sandwich the layers together with the nut-flavored buttercream. Spread two-thirds of the remaining plain buttercream around the side of the cake. Sprinkle the remaining chopped nuts on a sheet of foil and roll the side of the cake in the nuts to coat.

7 Spread the remaining plain buttercream on top of the cake. Smooth over the top with a spatula then make a zig-zag pattern all over the surface using the rounded tip of the knife. Starting from the center, pull the knife tip to the cake edge through the icing and mark 12 portions. Decorate each portion with a piece of walnut and place the remaining 2 pieces in the center. Serve as soon as possible, or refrigerate uncovered, overnight, and then serve at room temperature.

Philadelphia carrot cake

Makes 16 pieces

1 cup all-purpose flour
1 teaspoon baking soda
1 teaspoon ground cinnamon
½ teaspoon salt
1⅓ cups packed brown sugar
¾ cup vegetable oil
2 large eggs
1⅓ cups finely grated carrot
extra oil, for greasing
FROSTING
1 package (3 oz) cream cheese
2 tablespoons softened butter
½ cup superfine sugar
few drops vanilla
1 canned pineapple ring, drained thoroughly and
finely chopped (optional)

1 Preheat the oven to 350°F. Lightly oil an 8 inch square cake pan, line sides and base with waxed paper, then oil the paper.
2 Sift the flour with the soda, the cinnamon and salt and reserve.
3 Put the sugar into a large bowl. Using an electric mixer, gradually beat in the oil, then the eggs, one at a time. Add the flour mixture and mix with a wooden spoon until evenly blended. Finally stir in the carrots, mixing well.
4 Pour the mixture into the prepared cake pan and bake in the oven for 1 hour 10 minutes, until risen and firm to the touch at the center. (The top will probably crack slightly.) Cover with waxed paper halfway through baking time to avoid overbrowning.
5 Cool the cake for 5 minutes, then invert onto a wire rack. Peel off the lining paper and leave the cake to cool completely.
6 Make the frosting: Put the cheese into a large bowl with the butter, sugar, vanilla and the pineapple, if using, and beat until well mixed.
7 Turn the cake the right way up and place on a large serving plate. Spread the frosting over the top. To serve, cut the cake in quarters, then cut each quarter in 4 squares.

English layer cake

Makes 8–10 slices

2 cups self-rising flour
pinch of salt
1 cup soft butter
1 cup superfine sugar
4 large eggs, lightly beaten
melted butter or vegetable oil, for greasing
FILLING
3–4 tablespoons red jam
⅔ cup heavy cream (optional)
superfine or confectioners' sugar, for topping

1 Preheat the oven to 350°F. Grease two 8 inch round layer cake pans. Line the base of each pan with waxed paper, then grease the paper.

2 Sift the flour with the salt and set aside. Using a wooden spoon, or a hand-held electric mixer, beat the butter and superfine sugar until pale and fluffy. Add the eggs a little at a time, beating thoroughly after each addition. When the eggs have all been incorporated, fold in the sifted flour, about one-third at a time, using a large metal spoon.

3 Divide the batter equally between the prepared pans and level each surface. Bake in the oven for 40–45 minutes until the cakes are well risen and springy to the touch at the center.

4 Let the cakes stand in the pans for 30 seconds, then invert on a wire rack and remove the lining paper. Turn the cakes the right way up and let cool completely.

5 Spread 1 cake with jam. If filling with cream, whip until thick, then spread it over the underside of the remaining cake. Sandwich the cakes together, then sift superfine or confectioners' sugar over the top.

6 Place the cake on a serving plate; serve immediately or keep in a cool place for up to 2 hours.

VARIATIONS

Lemon layer: Beat in the grated rind of 1 lemon before adding eggs. Sandwich the cakes together with 3–4 tablespoons lemon cheese. Spread the top with lemon cheese. Decorate with candied lemon slices.

Chocolate layer: Mix 1½ tablespoons unsweetened cocoa with 2 tablespoons hot water; let cool slightly, then beat into the mixture before adding the eggs. Sandwich the cakes together with jam and a layer of lightly whipped cream. To finish the cake sift a little confectioners' sugar over the top of the cake, then decorate by piping a lattice of melted semisweet chocolate over the top.

Orange layer: Beat in the grated rind

of 1 orange before adding the eggs. Sandwich the cakes with marmalade or cream. If liked, whip ⅔ cup of heavy cream until it will hold its shape; spread some of the cream over the top of the cake, then use the remainder to pipe rosettes around the edge. Top each rosette with a drained canned mandarin orange section. Fresh orange sections can be used but canned mandarins are daintier and juicier.

Coffee and hazelnut layer: Blend 2½ teaspoons instant coffee powder with 1 tablespoon boiling water; let cool slightly, then beat into the mixture before adding the eggs. Sandwich the cakes together with 3–4 tablespoons chocolate hazelnut spread. Cover the top with canned chocolate frosting and decorate with toasted skinned hazelnut kernels.

Coconut layer: Add 2–3 drops vanilla when beating in the eggs. Sandwich the cakes together with 3–4 tablespoons red cherry jam. Mix 1 cup sifted confectioners' sugar with 1 tablespoon warm water and use to ice the top of the cake. While the icing is still soft, scatter the top thickly with shredded coconut; arrange sliced candied cherries around the top edge.

Orange cream sponge

Makes one 8 inch cake

3 eggs
⅓ cup superfine sugar
¾ cup self-rising flour
vegetable oil, for greasing
FILLING AND DECORATION
1 package (3 oz) cream cheese
⅔ cup heavy cream
¾ cup confectioners' sugar, sifted
1½ teaspoons grated orange rind
6–8 orange twists

1 Preheat the oven to 350°F. Lightly grease two 8 inch layer cake pans, line their bases with waxed paper, then lightly grease the paper.

2 Put the eggs and sugar in a heat-proof bowl. Set the bowl over a pan of gently simmering water. Using a rotary whip or hand-held electric mixer, beat until the mixture is thick enough to hold the trail of the beaters for 3 seconds when the beaters are lifted.

3 Remove the bowl from the pan and beat for a few minutes more, until the mixture is cool. Sift one-third of the flour over the mixture, then fold it in with a large metal spoon. Add any remaining flour in the same way.

4 Divide the mixture equally between the prepared pans and spread it evenly by carefully tilting the pans. Bake immediately in the oven for 12–15 minutes, until the cakes are golden and springy to the touch.

5 Let cool for 1–2 seconds, then invert the pans onto a wire rack. Peel off the lining paper and let cool completely.

6 Make the icing: Work the cream cheese with 2 tablespoons of the cream until soft. Gradually add the confectioners' sugar, beating constantly. Stir in the orange rind. Finally whip the remaining cream and fold it into the icing. Use about one-third of the icing to sandwich the cake layers together and spread the remaining orange cream over the top and side of the cake, covering it completely. Place on a serving plate, decorate with orange twists and serve as soon as possible.

Corn oil lemon cake

Makes one 8 inch cake

1½ cups all-purpose flour
pinch of salt
1 teaspoon baking powder
grated rind of 1 lemon
⅔ cup superfine sugar
½ cup corn oil
⅓ cup water
2 large eggs, separated
4 tablespoons lemon cheese
extra oil, for greasing
FROSTING
1 large egg white
¾ cup superfine sugar
pinch of salt
pinch of cream of tartar
1 tablespoon lemon juice
2 drops yellow food coloring (optional)

1 Preheat the oven to 350°F. Grease two 8 inch layer cake pans. Sift the flour, salt and baking powder into a bowl. Add the lemon rind and sugar and toss with your fingers. Make a well in the center.

2 Beat the oil, water and the egg yolks together and pour them into the well. Beat the mixture with a wooden spoon. It will be fairly stiff.

3 Stiffly beat the egg whites and fold them in. Divide the mixture between the prepared pans and bake for 20 minutes or until the cakes are firm and have shrunk slightly from the side of the pans. Turn the cakes out onto wire racks to cool.

4 When the layers are cool, sandwich them together with the lemon cheese.

5 To make the frosting, combine the egg white, sugar, salt and cream of tartar in the top of a double boiler and, using a balloon whip, whip until they are light and frothy.

6 Place over simmering water. Stir in the lemon juice and food coloring, if liked, and continue whipping until the mixture stands in stiff peaks, about 6–8 minutes.

7 Take the pan off the heat and spread the lemon frosting over the top of the cake. Leave the frosting to set for 1 hour before serving.

Coffee fudge cake

Makes 8 slices

1½ cups self-rising flour
1½ teaspoons baking powder
¾ cup soft margarine
1 cup packed light brown sugar
3 eggs
1 tablespoon strong black coffee
2–3 tablespoons apricot jam, for filling
vegetable oil, for greasing
FUDGE FROSTING
1 tablespoon strong black coffee
2–4 tablespoons half-and-half
3 tablespoons soft margarine
few drops vanilla
1½ cups confectioners' sugar, sifted

1 Preheat the oven to 325°F. Grease two 8 inch layer cake pans. Base line each pan with waxed paper, then grease the paper.

2 Sift the flour and baking powder into a large bowl. Add margarine, brown sugar, eggs and black coffee and beat with a wooden spoon for 1–2 minutes until evenly mixed.

3 Divide batter equally between prepared pans and level each surface. Bake in the oven for 35–40 minutes, until springy to the touch.

4 Cool layers for 5 minutes, then remove from pans and peel off lining papers. Leave cakes on a wire rack to cool completely.

5 Sandwich cold cakes together with jam, then place on a wire rack with a plate underneath.

6 Make the frosting: Put the coffee, 2 tablespoons half-and-half, margarine and vanilla into a small, heavy-bottomed pan. Stir over low heat until the margarine has melted, then bring to a boil. Pour immediately onto the sifted confectioners' sugar and beat with a wooden spoon until blended. If the mixture is very stiff, beat in remaining half-and-half.

7 Quickly spread the frosting over the top and side of the cake. Mark in wedges while the frosting is still soft, then let stand for about 30 minutes to set. The cake is best served on the day it is frosted.

Bundt cake

Serves 12–16

6 squares (6 oz) semisweet chocolate
2 cups all-purpose flour
1 teaspoon baking powder
½ teaspoon baking soda
¼ teaspoon salt
¾ cup soft butter or margarine
1 cup superfine sugar
5 eggs, separated
⅓ cup orange marmalade
¾ cup milk
½ cup finely ground almonds
CHOCOLATE CUSTARD FILLING
½ cup semisweet chocolate pieces
¼ cup butter or margarine
2 eggs, lightly beaten
MOCHA BUTTERCREAM
½ cup soft butter or margarine
½ cup semisweet chocolate pieces, melted
4 cups confectioners' sugar, sifted
3–4 tablespoons strong black coffee

1 Preheat the oven to 375°F. Grease a 12 cup bundt pan or 10 inch tube pan. Prepare the cake: Melt chocolate; cool. Sift the flour, baking powder, soda and salt together; set aside.
2 Beat the butter in a mixing bowl until smooth. Add the sugar and beat until light and fluffy. Slowly beat in the egg yolks. Stir in the chocolate and marmalade. Fold in the flour mixture alternately with the milk.
3 Beat the egg whites until stiff. Stir about 1 cup into the batter to lighten it. Fold in the remaining whites and the almonds.
4 Pour into the pan. Bake for 40–45 minutes or until the top springs back when pressed. Cool the cake in the pan on a wire rack for 15 minutes. Remove from the pan and let cool.
5 Make the filling: Melt the chocolate and butter, stirring until smooth. Off heat, cool slightly, then beat in the eggs. Return to the heat and cook, beating constantly for 2–3 minutes, or until slightly thickened. Cool.
6 Make the buttercream: Beat the butter in a bowl until smooth. Beat in the chocolate and stir in the sugar. Add the coffee slowly, beating until a spreading consistency is achieved.
7 Cut the cake horizontally in 2 layers. Spread the bottom layer with filling. Top with the second layer. Spread buttercream all over the cake and chill until ready to serve.

Strawberry roll

Makes 6 slices

3 large eggs
⅓ cup superfine sugar
¼ teaspoon almond extract
¾ cup all-purpose flour
melted fat or vegetable oil, for greasing
FILLING AND DECORATION
⅔ cup heavy cream
¼ teaspoon almond extract
1 large egg white
¼ cup superfine sugar
**1 cup crushed fresh strawberries or 1 can (8 oz) strawberries,
drained and crushed**
confectioners' sugar, sifted, for dredging
sliced strawberries, to decorate

1 Preheat the oven to 425°F. Grease a 13 × 9 inch jelly roll pan; line the pan with waxed paper. Grease the paper.
2 Put eggs, sugar and almond extract in a heatproof bowl. Set the bowl over a pan half full of simmering water.
3 Using a rotary whip, beat together until the mixture is thick and foamy. Continue until thick enough to hold the trail of the beaters for 3 seconds.
4 Remove the bowl from the pan and beat for a few minutes more until the mixture is cool. Sift one-third of the flour over the mixture, then fold it in with a large metal spoon. Add the remaining flour in the same way.
5 Pour the sponge batter into the prepared pan and spread evenly. Bake the cake immediately in the oven for 7–10 minutes until the surface is golden and springy to the touch.
6 While the cake is baking, lay a sheet of waxed paper on top of a clean, damp dish towel. Sift confectioners' sugar thickly over the paper.
7 Invert the baked cake onto the sugared paper. Peel off the paper. Trim the edge of the cake, then make a shallow cut along one short end, ½ inch from the edge. Loosely roll up the cake, with the sugared paper inside. Place the roll seam-side down on a wire rack and let cool.
8 Whip the cream and almond extract until thick. Beat the egg white to soft peaks. Beat in the superfine sugar, 1 tablespoon at a time, and continue beating until the meringue is stiff. Fold the meringue into the whipped cream, then fold in the strawberries.
9 Unroll the cake and remove the paper. Spread the filling over the cake, then gently roll it up again. Cover. Refrigerate for at least 30 minutes.
10 Sift confectioners' sugar over and decorate. Serve the day it is made.

Chocolate roll

Serves 6

**4 squares (4 oz) semisweet chocolate
4 large eggs, separated
½ cup superfine sugar
1 cup heavy cream
⅓ cup light cream
1 tablespoon chocolate liqueur (optional)
confectioners' sugar, sifted, for sprinkling
butter, for greasing**

1 Preheat the oven to 350°F. Line a 15 × 10 inch jelly roll pan with silicone treated paper or with greased waxed paper.
2 Break the chocolate in pieces and put it in a bowl with 3 tablespoons water. Set the bowl over simmering water. Stir from time to time until the chocolate is melted.
3 In a bowl beat the egg yolks until they are light and fluffy. Add the sugar slowly, continuing to beat. In a separate bowl beat the egg whites until they form stiff peaks.
4 Add the melted chocolate mixture to the beaten egg yolks, stirring it in thoroughly. Take a spoonful of the beaten whites and fold it into the yolk mixture to lighten it a little. Now very gently fold in the rest of the whites. Pour the mixture into the prepared pan, spreading it evenly. Bake for 15 minutes until the surface is springy.

5 Remove from the oven and cover the crisp top of the cake with a clean damp cloth: this will make the cake easier to roll. Let cool – leave overnight if possible.
6 Shake some sifted confectioners' sugar over a clean dish towel and turn the baked sponge onto the dish towel. Carefully peel off the paper, which will now be on top. The cake is very fragile, so ease the paper off.
7 Whip the creams together with the liqueur, if using. (You can add a little sugar if you like.) Spread the whipped cream over the surface of the sponge, taking great care not to tear it.
8 Using the dish towel as a guide, gently lift the longer edge of the cake up until it rolls over. Continue until the roll is completed. Sprinkle with confectioners' sugar and serve.

Cookies, Small Cakes & Traybakes

Cookies and small cakes are always firm favorites and in this chapter we've gathered together some delicious, melt-in-the-mouth morsels which you can serve with coffee, tea, as dessert or packed into a lunchbox as a special treat. Some of the cakes gathered here have a traditional flavor, such as Scottish shortbread, Parkin and Crunchy gingersnaps. Others have a continental touch – you can go French with our mouth-watering Madeleines and tuck into fruit-filled, chocolate-coated Florentines. For lovers of all-American cheesecake there are individual Cheesecake cookies – an unusual way of serving this delicious dessert.

Butterfly cakes

Makes 12

1¼ cups self-rising flour
pinch of salt
⅓ cup soft butter or margarine
⅓ cup superfine sugar
grated rind of 1 large orange
1 egg, beaten
2 tablespoons orange juice
BUTTERCREAM
½ cup soft butter or margarine
1½–2 cups confectioners' sugar, sifted
about 2 tablespoons orange juice
few drops of orange food coloring (optional)

1 Preheat the oven to 400°F. Line each mold of an individual cupcake pan with a cupcake paper or use double cupcake papers on a baking sheet.
2 Sift the flour with the salt and reserve. Beat the butter, sugar and orange rind together until pale and fluffy, then beat in the egg, a little at a time. Using a large metal spoon, fold in the sifted flour, then mix in the orange juice.
3 Divide the batter equally among the cupcake papers. Bake in the oven, above the center, for about 15 minutes, until golden and springy to the touch. Remove from the molds and let cool on a wire rack.

4 Meanwhile, make the buttercream: Beat the butter until very soft and creamy. Gradually beat in all but 1 teaspoon of the confectioners' sugar, adding enough orange juice to give a smooth buttercream which will hold its shape. Tint pale orange with a few drops of food coloring if liked. Put into a pastry bag fitted with a star tip.
5 Cut a horizontal slice from the top of each cake. Cut the slices in half and reserve.
6 Pipe a large rosette of buttercream on each cake, then replace the cake slices at an angle on the buttercream to resemble butterflies' wings. Sift the reserved confectioners' sugar over the top of the cakes.

Cheesecake cookies

Makes 16

½ cup packed light brown sugar
1½ cups all-purpose flour
¾ cup chopped walnuts
⅓ cup melted butter
1 package (8 oz) cream cheese
⅓ cup sugar
1 large egg, beaten
1 tablespoon lemon juice
2 tablespoons milk
1 teaspoon vanilla
butter or margarine, for greasing

1 Heat the oven to 350°F. Grease an 8 inch square cake pan. Combine the brown sugar, flour and nuts in a large bowl. Stir in the butter and mix with your hands until the mixture is light and crumbly.

2 Reserve one-third of the mixture. Place the remainder in the prepared pan and press down firmly. Bake for 15 minutes.

3 Meanwhile, beat the cream cheese and sugar together in a large bowl until smooth. Beat in the egg, lemon juice, milk and vanilla.

4 Pour the filling over the baked crust, top with the reserved crumbs, return to the oven and bake for 25 minutes.

5 Let cool in the pan, then cut in 16 squares and remove from the pan. Store in an airtight container in the refrigerator for up to 2 days.

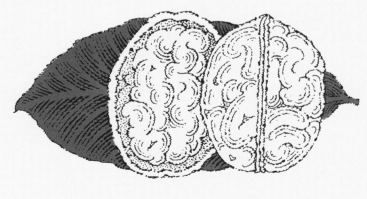

Scottish shortbread

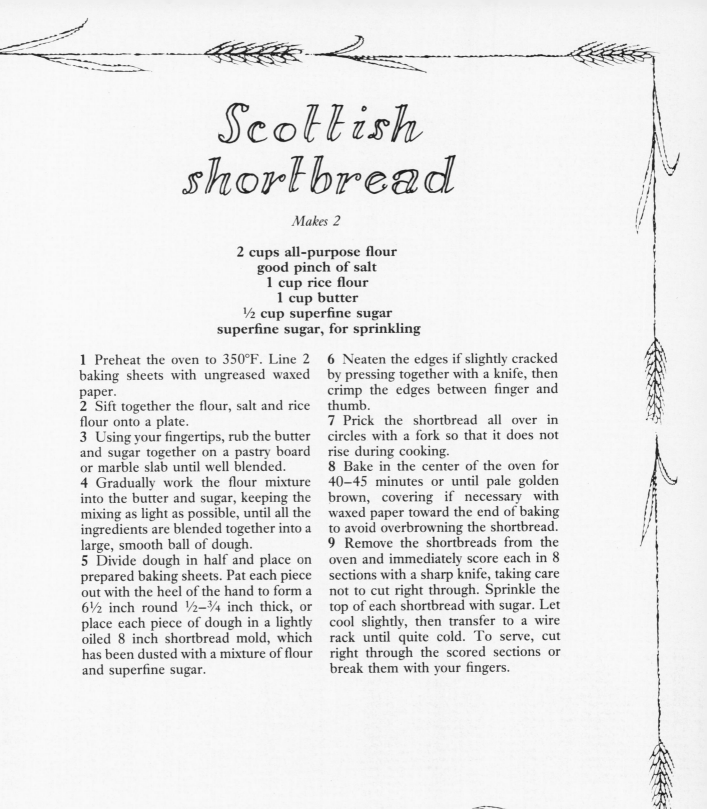

Makes 2

2 cups all-purpose flour
good pinch of salt
1 cup rice flour
1 cup butter
½ cup superfine sugar
superfine sugar, for sprinkling

1 Preheat the oven to 350°F. Line 2 baking sheets with ungreased waxed paper.
2 Sift together the flour, salt and rice flour onto a plate.
3 Using your fingertips, rub the butter and sugar together on a pastry board or marble slab until well blended.
4 Gradually work the flour mixture into the butter and sugar, keeping the mixing as light as possible, until all the ingredients are blended together into a large, smooth ball of dough.
5 Divide dough in half and place on prepared baking sheets. Pat each piece out with the heel of the hand to form a 6½ inch round ½–¾ inch thick, or place each piece of dough in a lightly oiled 8 inch shortbread mold, which has been dusted with a mixture of flour and superfine sugar.

6 Neaten the edges if slightly cracked by pressing together with a knife, then crimp the edges between finger and thumb.
7 Prick the shortbread all over in circles with a fork so that it does not rise during cooking.
8 Bake in the center of the oven for 40–45 minutes or until pale golden brown, covering if necessary with waxed paper toward the end of baking to avoid overbrowning the shortbread.
9 Remove the shortbreads from the oven and immediately score each in 8 sections with a sharp knife, taking care not to cut right through. Sprinkle the top of each shortbread with sugar. Let cool slightly, then transfer to a wire rack until quite cold. To serve, cut right through the scored sections or break them with your fingers.

Chocolate chip cookies

Makes about 30

½ cup plus 1 tablespoon soft butter
½ cup sugar
½ cup packed light brown sugar
1 egg
½ teaspoon vanilla
1½ cups all-purpose flour
½ teaspoon salt
½ teaspoon baking soda
½ cup chopped walnuts
⅔ cup semisweet chocolate chips

1 Preheat the oven to 375°F. With 1 tablespoon of butter, grease a baking sheet.
2 In a mixing bowl, beat the remaining butter until soft. Mix the sugars together and add them gradually to the butter, beating until the mixture is smooth and fluffy. Beat in the egg and vanilla.
3 Sift the flour with the salt and soda. Stir it into the butter-and-sugar mixture and mix to a smooth batter. Stir in the nuts and chocolate chips.
4 Drop the batter, about a teaspoon at a time, onto the baking sheet, leaving about a 1 inch space between each cookie.
5 Bake the cookies for 10 to 15 minutes or until they are lightly browned. Remove the baking sheet from the oven and transfer the cookies to a wire rack and leave to cool.

Madeleines

Makes about 12

¼ cup butter
2 large eggs, separated
¼ cup superfine sugar
½ cup all-purpose flour, sifted
rind of ½ lemon, finely grated

24

1 Preheat the oven to 375°F. Warm the butter until it is just soft enough to pour. Do not let it turn oily.

2 Place the egg yolks and sugar in a bowl and beat until pale and thick. Fold in the flour, lemon rind and butter until evenly blended. Beat the egg whites until stiff and fold in.

3 Spoon the mixture into greased and floured fluted madeleine molds or shallow muffin pans. Bake in the oven for about 9 minutes, or until the cakes are pale golden brown and firm to the touch. Cool them on a wire rack and serve them Parisien-style with café filtre or a pot of hot chocolate.

Lemon Jumbles

Makes 16

½ cup soft butter or margarine
⅔ cup superfine sugar
grated rind of ½ lemon
1 egg yolk, lightly beaten
1½ cups all-purpose flour, sifted
½ cup finely ground almonds
butter or margarine, for greasing
ICING
¾–1 cup confectioners' sugar
1 tablespoon strained lemon juice
few drops of yellow food coloring (optional)

1 Preheat the oven to 350°F. Grease a baking sheet. Beat the margarine, superfine sugar and lemon rind together until pale and fluffy. Add the egg yolk, a little at a time, beating thoroughly.

2 Using a metal spoon, work in the flour and almonds to make a firm dough. Place on a lightly floured surface. Knead for 1–2 minutes, until smooth.

3 Cut the dough in 8 equal pieces. With your hands, roll out each piece to a sausage shape, about 8 inches long and ¾ inch thick. Cut each roll across in half, then trim the ends.

4 Place the rolls on the prepared baking sheet, spacing them apart, then form each into an "S" shape. Bake in the oven for 12–15 minutes.

5 Leave the cookies to "settle" for 1–2 minutes, then ease them off the baking sheet with a spatula. Transfer to a wire rack and let cool completely.

6 Make the icing: Sift the confectioners' sugar into a bowl, then stir in enough lemon juice to give a smooth, thick consistency. Tint pale yellow with coloring, if liked.

7 Place a baking sheet underneath the wire rack. Trickle the icing over the cookies. Leave to set before serving.

Maids of honor

Makes 12

½ package (17¼ oz size) frozen puff pastry, thawed
FILLING
¼ cup cottage cheese
¼ cup superfine sugar
2 egg yolks
1 tablespoon melted butter
3 tablespoons finely ground almonds
2 teaspoons brandy or milk

1 Preheat the oven to 400°F.

2 On a lightly floured surface, roll out the pastry very thinly and cut out as many rounds as possible with a 3½ inch plain cookie cutter.

3 Layer the pastry trimmings on top of each other, roll out thinly and cut out more rounds. You should make 12 pastry rounds altogether.

4 Use the pastry rounds to line 12 individual pie pans. Prick pastry bases well in several places with a fork then place the pie pans in the refrigerator.

5 Strain the cheese into a bowl. Using a wooden spoon, work in the sugar, egg yolks and butter. Stir in almonds and brandy, mixing well.

6 Divide the filling equally among the pastry cases (they should only be one-third full). Bake the tarts in the oven for about 25 minutes, or until the filling is well risen and just firm to the touch.

7 Cool the tarts in the pans for 2–3 minutes, then transfer to a wire rack. Serve warm.

Macaroons

Makes 18

1½ cups finely ground almonds
¾ cup superfine sugar
few drops of almond extract
few drops of vanilla
2 small egg whites, lightly beaten
blanched almonds, to decorate
extra superfine sugar, for sprinkling

1 Preheat the oven to 350°F. Line 2 baking sheets with parchment paper.

2 Put the finely ground almonds and superfine sugar into a bowl and mix together well with a wooden spoon. Add the flavorings, then gradually stir in just enough egg white to give a fairly stiff consistency.

3 Put the mixture into a pastry bag fitted with a ½ inch plain tip. Pipe nine 1½ inch rounds onto each sheet. Alternatively, simply put heaped tablespoons of the mixture onto the baking sheet. Space rounds well apart, away from the edges of the baking sheets, to allow for spreading.

4 Place 1 almond in center of each round; sprinkle lightly with superfine sugar. Bake in the oven for 10–15 minutes, until just firm and beginning to color.

5 Cool the macaroons for 1–2 minutes, then transfer to wire racks and let cool completely. Peel the parchment paper from the macaroons. Serve at once, or store for up to 5 days.

Parkin cookies

Makes 12

½ cup all-purpose flour
½ teaspoon baking soda
1 teaspoon ground ginger
¼ teaspoon ground cinnamon
½ cup medium oatmeal
¼ cup diced margarine
¼ cup sugar
1 tablespoon light corn syrup
⅓ cup milk
2 tablespoons candied peel, to finish (optional)
margarine, for greasing

1 Preheat the oven to 350°F. Grease a large baking sheet.

2 Sift the flour, soda and spices into a bowl, then stir in the oatmeal. Add the margarine and rub it in with your fingertips until the mixture resembles fine bread crumbs. Stir in the sugar, syrup and milk, then gather together to a soft dough.

3 Divide the dough in 12 equal pieces. Using your hands, roll each piece into a ball, then place well apart on the prepared baking sheet. Put a little candied peel on the top of each one if liked, then flatten slightly with the back of a fork.

4 Bake in the oven for 10–15 minutes, until set and light golden in color. Cool the cookies for 5 minutes, then loosen from the baking sheet with a spatula and transfer carefully to a wire rack. Let cool completely.

Coconut kisses

Makes 18–20

2 egg whites
½ cup superfine sugar
2½–3 cups shredded coconut
about 6 candied cherries, roughly chopped

1 Preheat the oven to 300°F. Line a baking sheet with non-stick parchment paper.
2 Beat the egg whites in a clean, dry bowl to stiff peaks.
3 Using a metal spoon, gently fold in the superfine sugar, followed by the coconut, to give a stiff mixture.
4 Put spoonfuls of the mixture onto the prepared baking sheet, then form them into rocky shapes using 2 forks. Decorate with 1 or 2 small pieces of candied cherry.
5 Bake in the oven for about 30 minutes until dry and firm. Remove from the paper and cool on a wire rack. Serve immediately in cupcake papers, if liked.

Flapjacks

Makes 10–12

⅓ cup butter or margarine
3 tablespoons light corn syrup
⅔ cup light brown sugar
½ cup jumbo oats
½ cup rolled oats
butter or oil for greasing

1 Preheat oven to 350°F. Lightly brush an 8 inch square pan with melted butter or oil.
2 Cut the butter in small pieces and place in a heavy-bottomed saucepan. Add the syrup and sugar and place the saucepan over a low heat, mixing and stirring constantly with a wooden spoon until the butter has melted and the sugar has just dissolved.
3 Off heat, stir in the oats, and mix well. Spoon the mixture into the prepared pan and level the surface with the back of a metal spoon.
4 Bake in the center of the oven for 20 minutes, until the top is golden brown.
5 Place the pan on a wooden board and cut the bake into 10–12 wedges. Leave the flapjacks in the pan until completely cold before removing.

Honey nut brownies

Makes 16

2 squares (2 oz) semisweet chocolate, roughly chopped
½ cup butter
½ cup honey
2 eggs
1 teaspoon vanilla
1½ cups all-purpose flour
¾ teaspoon baking powder
½ teaspoon salt
3 tablespoons unsweetened cocoa
½ cup chopped walnuts
vegetable oil, for greasing

1 Preheat the oven to 325°F. Grease an 8 inch square cake pan.
2 Put the chocolate and butter in a heatproof bowl. Set the bowl over a pan half full of simmering water and leave, stirring occasionally, until the chocolate has melted. Remove from the heat and let cool slightly.
3 Put the honey, eggs and vanilla in a bowl and add the melted mixture. Beat the ingredients together with a fork.
4 Sift the flour, baking powder, salt and unsweetened cocoa into the bowl and beat together. Stir in the walnuts.
5 Pour the mixture into the prepared pan and spread out evenly.
6 Bake for 25–35 minutes or until a skewer inserted comes out clean.
7 Cool the brownies in the cake pan, then cut in squares.

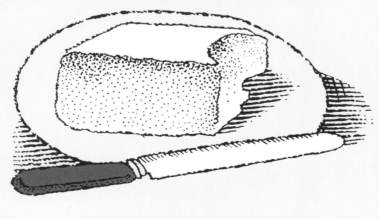

Crunchy gingersnaps

Makes about 30

2 cups Graham flour
1½ teaspoons ground ginger
1 teaspoon baking soda
½ cup soft margarine
½ cup packed light brown sugar
1 egg, lightly beaten
1 tablespoon honey
⅓ cup shredded coconut
2 tablespoons fine oatmeal
margarine, for greasing

1 Preheat the oven to 350°F. Lightly grease 2 baking sheets.
2 Sift the flour with the ginger and soda and reserve.
3 In a large bowl, beat the margarine and sugar together until light and fluffy. Add the egg, a little at a time, beating vigorously after each addition. Beat in the honey. With a large metal spoon, gradually fold in the flour, followed by the coconut and oatmeal.

4 Divide the mixture into 30 equal pieces and shape each into a round between the palms of your hands. Place rounds on prepared baking sheets, spacing them well apart.
5 Mark each cookie with the prongs of a fork, then bake in the oven for 10–15 minutes, until golden brown.
6 Allow cookies to "settle" for about 1 minute. Transfer to a wire rack and let cool completely.

Hazelnut florentines

Makes 20

⅓ cup butter
½ cup packed light brown sugar
1 cup finely chopped hazelnuts
½ cup quartered candied cherries
2 tablespoons finely chopped candied peel
butter for greasing
7 squares (7 oz) semisweet chocolate

1 Preheat the oven to 350°F. Melt the butter and sugar together in a saucepan and bring gently to a boil.
2 Remove the pan from the heat and stir in the hazelnuts, cherries and candied peel.
3 Cover 2 baking sheets with buttered waxed paper. Place 2 teaspoon portions of the mixture, well apart, on the baking sheets and flatten them slightly.
4 Bake for 10 minutes. The mixture will spread out considerably, so cut each florentine into a perfect round with a 3 inch cookie cutter while they are still warm and flexible. Cool the cookies slightly, then, with a spatula, lift them from the sheets and lay them, smooth side up, on a clean sheet of waxed paper.
5 Break up the chocolate and put it in the top part of a double boiler or a bowl set over a pan of hot, not boiling, water. Melt the chocolate over a low heat.
6 Using a pastry brush, brush a thin layer of melted chocolate over the smooth side of each florentine. Leave to set, and keep the remaining chocolate warm.
7 Brush all the remaining chocolate over the cookies and leave until they are completely set.

Cut & come~again cakes

The cakes collected here will certainly have your family and friends coming again for more. Full of healthy, wholesome ingredients these cakes are ideal for those who would rather avoid creamy creations. There are the great standbys — perfect for those times when neighbors call for coffee or friends drop in. Most of these cakes will keep for a week if stored in an airtight container; rich Dundee cake, packed full of fruit and topped with whole almonds, can be kept for up to a month during which time its flavors will gradually mature and its texture will become even more moist.

Saffron honey cake

Makes 8 slices

6 saffron strands
¼ cup milk
1½ cups all-purpose flour
1 tablespoon baking powder
½ cup soft butter or margarine
½ cup superfine sugar
2 tablespoons honey
2 eggs, lightly beaten
⅓ cup cut mixed candied peel
½ cup golden raisins
vegetable oil, for greasing
ICING
10 saffron strands
1 tablespoon boiling water
1½ cups confectioners' sugar
1–2 tablespoons lemon juice

1 Preheat the oven to 350°F. Grease a deep 8 inch round cake pan, line side and base with waxed paper; grease paper.
2 Crush the 6 saffron strands for the cake between your fingers and put into a small, heavy-bottomed saucepan with the milk. Bring just to a boil, then remove from heat and leave to stand for 20 minutes.
3 Sift the flour with the baking powder and reserve.
4 Beat the butter, sugar and honey until pale and fluffy. Beat in the eggs, a little at a time, adding 1 tablespoon sifted flour if mixture shows signs of curdling. Fold in the sifted flour.
5 Strain the saffron milk, then stir into cake mixture, 1 tablespoon at a time. Fold in the candied peel and golden raisins. Spoon mixture into the prepared pan and then level surface.
6 Bake in oven for 65 minutes, or until a warmed fine skewer inserted into the center comes out clean.
7 Meanwhile, put the 10 saffron strands for the icing into a small bowl with the boiling water.
8 Let the cake cool for 5 minutes and peel off the lining paper. Turn cake right way up and leave it on a wire rack to cool completely.
9 Sift the confectioners' sugar into a large bowl and stir in 1 tablespoon lemon juice. Strain the saffron water, then stir into the icing until evenly colored. Stir in the remaining lemon juice if necessary, to give a thick pouring consistency.
10 Place a large plate under the rack. Pour icing over cake, smooth with a slim spatula and leave to set.

Spiced peanut cake

Makes 12 squares

⅔ cup shelled, unsalted peanuts
1 cup margarine, plus extra for greasing
1¼ cups packed dark brown sugar
2 cups Graham flour
2 teaspoons baking powder
2 teaspoons apple pie spice
4 large eggs, beaten
¼ cup milk

1 Preheat the oven to 350°F. Grease an 11 × 7 inch cake pan.
2 Grind the peanuts finely in a blender or food processor.
3 In a large bowl, cream the margarine and beat in the sugar. Stir together the flour, baking powder and apple pie spice and beat this into the margarine alternately with the eggs.

4 Beat in the milk, then the peanuts. Pour the batter into the prepared pan and bake for about 30 minutes, or until the cake is firm in the center and has shrunk away slightly from the side of the pan.
5 Cool in the pan for 10 minutes, then invert onto a wire rack to cool completely. Cut into 12 squares.

Island apple cake

Makes 6–8 slices

2½ cups self-rising flour
2 teaspoons ground cinnamon
1 cup packed light brown sugar
1 cup seedless raisins
½ cup vegetable oil
2 eggs, lightly beaten
¾ cup hard cider
vegetable oil, for greasing
TOPPING
1–2 tart cooking apples, preferably Rhode Island Greenings,
pared, cored, halved and sliced
lemon cheese, to glaze

1 Preheat the oven to 350°F. Lightly grease an 8 inch springform pan. Line the side and base with waxed paper, then lightly grease the paper with vegetable oil.

2 Sift the flour and cinnamon into a large bowl. Add the sugar, raisins, oil, eggs and cider and beat together with a wooden spoon until evenly mixed.

3 Pour the batter into the prepared pan. Arrange the apple slices over the top. Bake in the oven for about 1½ hours, until a fine, warmed skewer inserted in the center comes out clean. Cover with waxed paper during baking if the apples show signs of over-browning.

4 Let the cake cool for 5 minutes, then remove from the pan and peel off the lining paper. Place the right way up on a wire rack. Brush the apples with lemon cheese, then let the cake cool.

Gingerbread

Makes 16 squares

¾ cup margarine
½ cup light corn syrup
½ cup dark corn syrup
1⅓ cups packed dark brown sugar
4 cups all-purpose flour
1 tablespoon ground ginger
1 tablespoon baking powder
1 teaspoon baking soda
1 teaspoon salt
1 egg, lightly beaten
1¼ cups milk
melted margarine, for greasing

1 Preheat the oven to 350°F. Grease a deep 9 inch square loose-bottomed cake pan. Line the side and base with waxed paper, then grease the paper.

2 Put the margarine, syrups, and sugar into a heavy-bottomed saucepan and place over very low heat, stirring, until the margarine has just melted. Let cool slightly.

3 Meanwhile, sift the flour, ginger, baking powder, soda and salt into a bowl, then make a well in the center.

4 Add the egg, milk and melted mixture to the dry ingredients and mix with a wooden spoon until smoothly blended. Pour into the prepared pan and bake in the oven for about 1½ hours, until just firm to the touch.

5 Let cool for 20 minutes, then remove from the pan and peel off the lining paper. Leave on a wire rack to cool completely. Wrap in foil and store in an airtight tin for 1 week before cutting the gingerbread.

Pound cake

Makes 12 slices

1 cup all-purpose flour
1 cup self-rising flour
pinch of salt
¾ cup soft butter (no substitute)
¾ cup superfine sugar
1 teaspoon vanilla
3 large eggs, lightly beaten
2 tablespoons milk
2 thin slices candied citron peel
vegetable oil, for greasing

1 Preheat the oven to 325°F. Grease a deep 8 inch round cake pan, line the side and base with waxed paper, then lightly grease the paper.

2 Sift the flours with the salt.

3 In a separate bowl, beat the butter and sugar until very pale and fluffy, then beat in the vanilla. Add the eggs, a little at a time, beating thoroughly after each addition.

4 Using a large metal spoon, fold in the sifted flours, then stir in the milk. Spoon the batter into the prepared pan and level the surface.

5 Bake the cake in the oven for 1 hour, then remove from the oven and carefully arrange the citron peel on the top. (The top may have cracked slightly.) Return to the oven for a further 15 minutes, or until firm to the touch and a warmed fine skewer inserted into the center of the pound cake comes out quite clean.

6 Cool the cake for 10–15 minutes, then turn out of the pan and peel off the lining paper. Place the cake the right way up on a wire rack and let cool completely before serving.

Pineapple & ginger cake

Serves 6

1 cup self-rising flour
1 teaspoon baking powder
½ cup soft margarine
⅓ cup superfine sugar
2 large eggs
¼ cup finely chopped preserved ginger
melted margarine, for greasing
TOPPING
2 tablespoons margarine
½ cup packed light brown sugar
1 can (8 oz) pineapple rings, drained
1 piece preserved ginger
angelica, cut in "leaves"

1 Preheat the oven to 325°F. Grease a deep 8 inch cake pan with melted margarine, then line the base with a foil round.

2 Make the topping: Melt the margarine in a small pan, add the brown sugar and stir over gentle heat until the sugar has melted. Spread the mixture over the base of the pan.

3 Pat the pineapple rings dry with kitchen paper towels, then halve them and arrange on the sugar mixture in a decorative design. Slice the piece of preserved ginger. Put one piece in the semi-circle of each halved pineapple ring and one in the center. Arrange leaves of angelica around the edge and in the center.

4 Make the cake: Sift the flour and baking powder into a bowl. Add the margarine, superfine sugar, eggs and chopped preserved ginger and beat together with a wooden spoon for 2–3 minutes, until pale and fluffy. Spoon the mixture carefully into the pan and level the surface with a spatula.

5 Bake in the oven for 1 hour 10 minutes, until the cake is springy to the touch at the center and is shrinking slightly from the side of the pan.

6 Cool the cake in the pan for 5 minutes, then run a slim spatula around the edge and invert on a wire rack. Carefully peel off the foil, let cool completely, then transfer to a serving platter. Serve as soon as possible.

Chunky apple cake

Makes 6–8 slices

2 cups all-purpose flour
2 teaspoons baking powder
½ teaspoon ground allspice
¼ teaspoon freshly grated nutmeg (optional)
½ cup soft butter or margarine
1 cup packed light brown sugar
2 eggs, beaten
⅓ cup golden raisins
3 cups diced tart apples
2 tablespoons dark brown sugar
vegetable oil, for greasing

1 Preheat the oven to 350°F. Grease a deep 8 inch round springform pan. Line the side and base with waxed paper, then grease the paper.

2 Sift the flour into a bowl. Sift the baking powder, allspice and nutmeg, if using, then stir to mix thoroughly.

3 Beat together the margarine and light brown sugar until it becomes pale and fluffy.

4 Add the eggs to the margarine and sugar, a little at a time, beating thoroughly after each addition. If the mixture begins to curdle, add 1 tablespoon flour mixture with the next addition of egg.

5 Using a large metal spoon, fold in the flour mixture, followed by the golden raisins and two-thirds of the diced apples. Spoon into the prepared pan and level the top.

6 Scatter the remaining apples evenly over the surface, then sprinkle over the dark brown sugar. Bake the cake in the oven for about 1½ hours, until the top is firm at the center. Cover with waxed paper after approximately 1 hour to prevent scorching.

7 Let the cake cool for 10 minutes, then remove from the pan and peel off the lining paper. Leave on a wire rack to cool completely.

Dundee cake

Makes 16 slices

2 cups all-purpose flour
¼ teaspoon salt
½ cup finely ground almonds
⅔ cup dried currants
⅔ cup golden raisins
⅔ cup seedless raisins
½ cup candied cherries, rinsed, dried and chopped
⅓ cup chopped mixed candied peel
1 cup soft butter
1 cup packed light brown sugar
finely grated rind of 1 orange
finely grated rind of 1 lemon
4 eggs, lightly beaten
1 tablespoon sherry, brandy, orange juice or milk
¼ cup whole blanched almonds
vegetable oil, for greasing

1 Preheat the oven to 300°F. Grease a deep 8 inch round cake pan, then line the base and side with a double thickness of waxed paper. Lightly grease the paper with oil.

2 Sift the flour and salt into a bowl and stir in the ground almonds. In a separate bowl, mix the dried fruits, cherries and peel. Set aside.

3 Beat the butter, sugar and grated orange and lemon rind until pale and fluffy. Beat in the eggs, a little at a time, then fold in the sifted flour alternately with the fruit mixture. Stir in the sherry.

4 Spoon the cake mixture into the prepared pan, level the surface, then arrange the almonds on the top. Bake for about 3 hours until browned and firm to the touch. Cover the cake with waxed paper if it browns too fast, but avoid opening the oven door for the first hour of cooking or the cake may sink.

5 Let the cake cool for 30 minutes, then remove from the pan and peel off the lining paper. Stand the cake the right way up on a wire rack and leave until cold. Store wrapped in foil in an airtight container.

Farmhouse Favorites

These cakes and bakes are regular fare down on the farm where freshly-made muffins, griddle cakes and drop biscuits, oozing with butter and home-made jam, await our country cousins as they troop in from the fields, appetites honed by the country air. With these farmhouse favorites you can bring the taste of the country to your own kitchen. Enjoy Singin' hinny, which is made in moments; rustle up some Tea biscuits, delicious served with cream and strawberry jam; or try your hand at Griddle cakes and Drop biscuits which you can cook in the skillet if you do not have a farmhouse-style range.

Cottage cakes

Makes 6–8

2 cups all-purpose flour
2 teaspoons baking powder
large pinch of salt
½ cup diced margarine or butter
½ cup cottage cheese, strained
2 teaspoons lemon juice
beaten egg white and superfine sugar, for glazing
FILLING
½ cup soft margarine or butter
2 teaspoons light brown sugar
2 teaspoons ground apple pie spice
1 cup dried currants
½ cup chopped mixed candied peel

1 Make the dough: Sift the flour, baking powder and salt into a bowl. Rub in the margarine. Stir in the cheese and lemon juice, then work to a soft dough with one hand.

2 Put the dough on a lightly floured surface and knead briefly until smooth. Roll out to a rectangle and mark the rectangle of dough across into 3 sections with a knife.

3 Fold the bottom section of the dough over the center, then fold the top section of the dough over the bottom one. Give the dough a quarter turn and roll out again. Fold in 3 again, then wrap and refrigerate for 30 minutes.

4 Meanwhile, make the filling: Beat the margarine with the sugar and spice until smooth and creamy, then mix in the dried currants and peel.

5 Preheat the oven to 400°F. Dampen a large baking sheet.

6 Roll out the dough fairly thinly on a lightly floured surface, then cut out as many rounds as possible, using a 5½ inch inverted saucer as a guide. Knead the trimmings together, roll out and cut out more rounds. You should make 6–8.

7 Divide the filling equally among the rounds, spooning it into the center. Dampen the edge of each round with water, then draw the dough up to enclose the filling and pinch to seal.

8 Turn the cakes over and flatten slightly by rolling over lightly with the rolling pin. Brush with egg white and sprinkle with sugar.

8 Make 3 slits in the tops with a knife, then transfer to the baking sheet. Bake for 15 minutes. Serve warm.

Drop biscuits

Makes 10

1 cup all-purpose flour
2 teaspoons baking powder
pinch of salt
1 large egg, lightly beaten
2 tablespoons honey
⅔ cup milk
vegetable oil or melted fat, to grease

1 Gently heat a griddle or a heavy skillet.
2 In a bowl sift together the flour, baking powder and salt. Stir in the egg and honey, then gradually pour over the milk, beating all the time. Beat until a smooth batter is formed.
3 Check that the griddle or skillet is hot enough by sprinkling it with flour; this should turn brown in 2–3 minutes. Brush the flour off, then grease with a little vegetable oil or melted fat.
4 Drop the mixture, 2 teaspoons at a time, in rounds well apart on the griddle. When the tops start to bubble, after about 3 minutes, flip them over with a slim spatula and cook the other side for a further 2–3 minutes.
5 Keep the biscuits warm in a clean, folded dish towel while you cook the remainder of the batter. Serve them warm, with butter.

Singin' hinny

Serves 8

2 cups self-rising flour
¼ teaspoon salt
½ teaspoon baking powder
⅓ cup diced shortening
2 tablespoons superfine sugar
⅓ cup dried currants
5–6 tablespoons milk
1–2 tablespoons shortening
butter, for serving

1 Sift the flour, salt and baking powder together. Add diced shortening and rub it into the flour with your fingertips for 2–3 minutes until the mixture resembles fine bread crumbs.

2 Mix in the sugar, dried currants and enough milk to make a fairly soft but manageable dough.

3 Roll out the dough on a lightly floured surface to a round about 8 inches in diameter. Cut in half, if liked, to make it easier to lift into the skillet.

4 Heat 1 tablespoon of the shortening in a large, heavy skillet. Put dough in pan and cook over low heat for 10–15 minutes. It should be cooked more than halfway through and be well browned underneath.

5 Lift the dough with a fish turner and add more shortening to the skillet, allowing it to melt and coat the base. Turn the hinny over, then gently lower it back into the skillet. Continue cooking the hinny very gently for about 10 minutes or until brown on the underside. Check during cooking and lower the heat more, if necessary, to prevent the hinny over-browning and burning.

6 Using a fish turner, remove the hinny to a working surface or board. Split it in half horizontally while it is hot and spread with butter. Sandwich together again and cut into wedges. Serve at once, while still hot.

Baking Powder biscuits

Makes 12

2 cups all-purpose flour
2 teaspoons baking powder
1 teaspoon salt
5 tablespoons shortening, butter or margarine
¾ cup milk

1 Preheat oven to 450°F.

2 Sift flour, baking powder and salt together into a large mixing bowl. Cut in the shortening and rub with your fingertips until the mixture resembles coarse crumbs.

3 Make a well in the center of the dry ingredients, pour in the milk. Stir with a fork to make a soft dough that just pulls away from the side of the bowl to form a ball.

4 Place the dough on lightly floured surface and knead about 10 strokes. Roll out or pat dough to ½ inch thickness. Cut it into rounds with a well-floured 2 inch round, straight or fluted biscuit cutter.

5 Place the biscuits on an ungreased baking sheet. Space them about 1 inch apart for crusty biscuits, or place them close together for soft-sided biscuits. Bake 12–15 minutes or until golden brown. Remove from the baking sheet with a spatula and serve piping hot.

Grandmother's doughnuts

Makes about 2½ dozen

3½ cups all-purpose flour
1 tablespoon baking powder
1 teaspoon ground cinnamon
½ teaspoon grated nutmeg
½ teaspoon salt
2 eggs
1 cup sugar
3 tablespoons vegetable oil or shortening
1 cup milk
vegetable oil for cooking
sifted confectioners' sugar

1 Sift flour, baking powder, cinnamon, nutmeg and salt together; set aside.

2 Beat the eggs in a large mixing bowl until foamy. Add the sugar, oil and milk and beat well. Add the flour mixture; beat with a hand-held electric mixer at low speed until well combined and smooth. Place the dough in a bowl and refrigerate for 2 hours.

3 Roll the dough out on a lightly floured surface to about ½ inch thickness. Cut dough with a floured doughnut cutter. Gather dough scraps, re-roll, and cut out as many additional doughnuts as possible.

4 Heat a depth of 3 or 4 inches of vegetable oil to 365°F in a deep-fat fryer or large Dutch oven. Lower 3 or 4 doughnuts at a time gently into the hot oil. Fry the doughnuts for 1 or 2 minutes or until they are golden brown. Turn carefully with a slotted spoon and fry 1 minute longer or until golden. Remove the doughnuts with a slotted spoon and place on kitchen paper towels to drain for about 2 minutes.

5 Place the confectioners' sugar in a small paper bag. Add 1 or 2 doughnuts at a time and gently shake the bag to coat the doughnuts.

VARIATIONS:

Wholewheat doughnuts: Follow the recipe above using 1½ cups wholewheat flour and 2 cups all-purpose flour. Do not sift flours. Stir flours and spices together until well combined. Proceed as directed above.

Chocolate doughnuts: Follow recipe above, but omitting cinnamon and nutmeg. Increase sugar to 1⅓ cups. Add 2 squares (2 oz) unsweetened chocolate, melted and cooled and 1 teaspoon vanilla along with milk. Proceed with the recipe as directed.

Buttermilk doughnuts: Follow the recipe above substituting buttermilk for milk. Decrease baking powder to 2 teaspoons and add 1 teaspoon baking soda to dry ingredients.

Crullers or twists: Prepare recipe above or buttermilk variation. Refrigerate dough. Roll dough out to about ¼ inch thickness and cut in strips about 6 to 7 inches long and ¾ inch wide. Let strips rest about 15 minutes. Twist strips 2 or 3 times and pinch ends. Fry as directed above.

Date & oatmeal muffins

Makes 16 small muffins

1 cup self-rising flour, sifted
1 teaspoon baking powder
pinch of salt
⅓ cup medium oatmeal
¼ cup superfine sugar
⅓ cup minced dates
1 tablespoon light corn syrup
1 tablespoon margarine or butter
⅔ cup milk
vegetable oil, for greasing

1 Preheat the oven to 400°F. Grease sixteen 2½ inch muffin pans.

2 Put the dry ingredients into a bowl with the dates and stir well to mix. Make a well in the center.

3 Stir the syrup, margarine and milk together in a saucepan over low heat until the fat has melted, then pour into the dry ingredients and beat until smoothly blended.

4 Divide the mixture equally among the prepared pans, then bake in the oven for 15–20 minutes until well-risen and springy.

5 Serve the muffins split and buttered while they are still warm.

Tollhouse rockies

Makes 12–14

**2 cups all-purpose flour
2 teaspoons baking powder
pinch of salt
½ cup margarine or butter
½ cup sugar
grated rind of 1 orange
½ cup chocolate chips
1 egg, lightly beaten
a little milk, to mix
melted fat or vegetable oil, for greasing**

1 Preheat the oven to 400°F. Lightly grease 2 baking sheets.
2 Sift the flour, baking powder and salt into a large bowl. Cut in the margarine then rub it in until the mixture resembles fine breadcrumbs.
3 Stir in the sugar, orange rind and chocolate chips. Using a fork, mix in the egg, then stir in just enough milk to make a moist but stiff mixture.

4 Using 2 forks, put the mixture onto the greased baking sheets in small rocky heaps. Make 12–14 heaps, spacing them well apart to allow for spreading.
5 Bake the cakes in the oven for about 30 minutes until risen and browned. Lift the baked cakes onto a wire rack with a fish turner or spatula and let cool. Serve fresh.

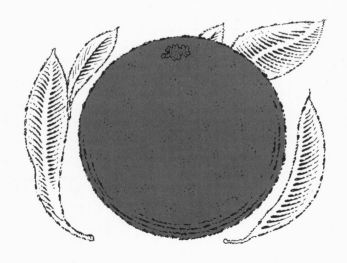

Filled tea biscuits

Makes 7–8

2 cups all-purpose flour
1 teaspoon cream of tartar
½ teaspoon baking soda
½ teaspoon salt
¼ cup diced margarine or butter
½–⅔ cup milk
vegetable oil, for greasing
extra all-purpose flour
TO SERVE
3–4 tablespoons strawberry jam
½ cup heavy cream, whipped

1 Preheat oven to 450°F. Grease and lightly flour a large baking sheet.
2 Sift the flour with the cream of tartar, soda and salt, then sift again into a large bowl. Add the diced margarine and rub it in until the mixture resembles fine bread crumbs. Make a well in the center.
3 Pour in most of the milk and mix to a soft (but not sticky) dough with a fork, adding a little more of the milk if necessary. Gather the dough into a ball, place it on a lightly floured surface and knead it lightly and briefly until smooth.
4 Either pat or lightly roll out the dough to a round about ½ inch thick.

Using a 2½ inch round biscuit cutter, cut out as many biscuits as possible. Lightly knead the trimmings together, pat or roll out again and cut out more biscuits.
5 Brush the tops of the biscuits with milk and place on the prepared baking sheet. Bake in the oven, just above the center, for about 15 minutes until risen and browned. Remove the biscuits from the oven, wrap in a clean dish towel and let cool.
6 To serve, split each biscuit in half with your fingers, spread the bottom half with jam and the top with whipped cream, then lightly replace the top half of each biscuit.

Cornbread muffins

Makes 12

1 cup yellow cornmeal
1½ cups all-purpose flour, sifted
¼ cup superfine sugar
2 teaspoons baking powder
1 teaspoon salt
1 large egg, lightly beaten
1 cup buttermilk
½ cup milk
¼ cup margarine or butter, melted
margarine, for greasing

1 Preheat the oven to 400°F. Brush 12 deep muffin pans lightly all over with margarine.
2 Sift the dry ingredients together into a bowl and make a well in the center.
3 Mix together the egg, buttermilk, milk and melted margarine and pour into the well. Using a balloon whip, combine swiftly with a few strokes.
4 Spoon the batter into the prepared pans, filling them two-thirds full. Bake in the oven for 15–20 minutes until golden.
5 Let the muffins cool slightly in the pans, then run a knife around the edge of the pans and invert them onto a wire rack. Serve the muffins warm.

Jam surprises

Makes 8

1¾ cups all-purpose flour
¼ cup rice flour
2 teaspoons baking powder
pinch of salt
⅓ cup diced margarine or butter
⅓ cup superfine sugar
1 egg
⅓ cup milk
2 tablespoons red jam or grape jelly
superfine sugar, for sprinkling
vegetable oil, for greasing

1 Preheat the oven to 400°F. Grease a large baking sheet and line the base with waxed paper; grease the paper.

2 Sift the flour, rice flour, baking powder and salt into a large bowl. Add the margarine and rub it in with your fingertips, then stir in the sugar. Make a well in the center. Beat the egg with the milk, then add to the dry ingredients and mix to a moist dough.

3 Cut the dough in 8 equal pieces. With lightly floured hands, shape each piece into a ball. Make a hollow in the center of each bun with your finger. Spoon a little jam into each hollow, then pinch the edges of the dough together to seal.

4 Place the buns, sealed side down, on the prepared baking sheet. Bake in the oven, just above center, for about 20 minutes, until risen, golden and just firm to the touch.

5 Cool the buns for 10–15 minutes, then transfer to a wire rack. Sprinkle with superfine sugar and let cool completely. Serve fresh.

Griddle cakes

Makes 12

**2 cups all-purpose flour
1 teaspoon baking soda
1 teaspoon cream of tartar
1 teaspoon salt
1 tablespoon margarine or butter
1 tablespoon superfine sugar
1¼ cups dairy sour cream
shortening, for greasing
butter, to serve**

1 Sift the flour, soda, cream of tartar and salt into a large bowl. Add the margarine and rub it in with your fingertips, then stir in the superfine sugar.

2 Using a fork, add enough sour cream to make a soft dough. Divide the dough in half, flour your hands lightly, then knead the dough lightly on a well-floured surface until smooth.

3 Carefully shape the dough into 2 rounds, each about ½ inch thick. Cut each round in 6 equal wedges.

4 Lightly grease a heavy skillet or griddle with shortening and heat over moderate heat.

5 Pour away any excess shortening from the skillet or griddle, then cook the cakes in batches for about 4–5 minutes on each side until golden and cooked through. Regrease the griddle with shortening as necessary.

6 Cool the cakes on a wire rack, for 20 minutes. Serve on the day of making, and spread each one generously with plenty of butter.

Quickbreads & Yeast Bakes

A sure sign of the country kitchen is the delicious smell of bread baking; nothing can beat the taste of hunks of warm bread, straight from the oven, served with lashings of butter. If you are new to bread-making this chapter has recipes which could not be more straightforward: Irish soda bread is simple to make as is Bara brith, a Welsh specialty, flavored with tea and spices. Children will love our Flowerpot loaf which is baked in a terracotta pot, and our recipe for Quick brown bread is guaranteed to be a winner.

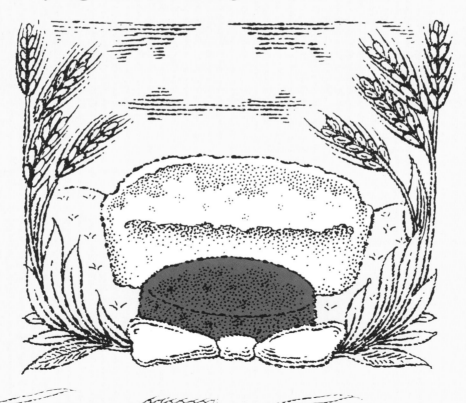

Currant bun ring

Makes 16 slices

¾ cup lukewarm milk
½ cup superfine sugar
1 package (¼ oz) active dry yeast
3 cups all-purpose flour
pinch of salt
⅓ cup diced butter
1 egg, beaten
¼ cup lukewarm water
1 teaspoon ground cinnamon
¼ cup chopped walnuts
¼ cup dried currants
extra butter, for greasing

1 Put the milk in a small bowl. Stir in 1 teaspoon of the sugar and sprinkle the active dry yeast on the top. Mix well. Set aside in a warm place for 15–20 minutes until frothy.

2 Sift the flour and salt into a large bowl. Rub in half the butter, then stir in half the remaining sugar. Make a well in the center, then pour in the egg, the yeast mixture and lukewarm water. Mix to a soft dough.

3 Put the dough on a lightly floured surface and knead for 10 minutes. Clean and grease the bowl. Put the dough into the bowl and turn it over to lightly grease the surface. Cover with greased plastic; leave in warm place for 1 hour, or until doubled in bulk.

4 Gently melt remaining butter in a small pan, then remove from heat. In a small bowl, mix remaining sugar with the cinnamon and walnuts. Grease a 1½ quart ring mold, then sprinkle in 4 teaspoons walnut mixture.

5 Put the dough on a lightly floured surface and knead in the dried currants. Divide into 36 equal pieces and roll each into a ball.

6 Place 12 balls in the base of the ring mold and sprinkle with one-third of the remaining walnut mixture. Add another row of balls and a further third of the walnut mixture. Top with the remaining balls. Making sure the balls of dough are firmly packed, brush with the remaining melted butter and sprinkle over the rest of the walnut mixture.

7 Cover and leave in a warm place for about 20 minutes, or until the dough has risen almost to the top of the mold. Preheat the oven to 400°F.

8 Uncover the mold and bake above center of oven for 10 minutes. Lower heat to 350°F and bake for 20 minutes.

9 Cool the loaf in the mold for 8–10 minutes. Meanwhile, increase oven heat to 450°F. Invert loaf on a baking sheet. Return to oven for 4–5 minutes to brown top. Let cool, then serve.

Shortening bread

Makes one 8 inch square bake

½ cake (⅗ oz) size compressed yeast
1 teaspoon sugar
⅔ cup lukewarm water
2 cups all-purpose flour
large pinch of salt
butter for greasing
1 tablespoon sugar, to glaze
FILLING
¼ cup shortening
¼ cup sugar
⅓ cup golden raisins

1 Cream the yeast with the sugar in a small bowl. Mix in the lukewarm water. Set aside for 10 minutes.

2 Sift the flour and salt into a large warmed bowl. Add the yeast mixture and mix to a soft dough. Knead for about 5 minutes, until smooth. Shape into a ball, place in the bowl, cover and leave in a warm place for about 45 minutes, or until doubled in bulk.

3 Roll out to an oblong about ¼ inch thick. To fill, dot half the shortening over the top two-thirds of the oblong and sprinkle the shortening with half the sugar and half the golden raisins. Fold the bottom third up and the top third down.

4 Give the dough a quarter turn and repeat the rolling, dotting and folding process using the remaining shortening, sugar and raisins.

5 Roll out and fold to fit a greased 8 inch square cake pan. Leave in a warm place to rise for about 30 minutes. Meanwhile, preheat the oven to 425°F.

6 For the glaze, dissolve the sugar in 1 tablespoon water and brush over the cake. Score the surface of the dough into squares and bake in the center of the oven for about 30 minutes, or until golden brown. Invert the bread and pour over it any juices. Shortening bread is best eaten warm.

Bara brith

Makes 2 × 2 lb loaves

1⅓ cups golden raisins
⅔ cup dried currants
⅔ cup seedless raisins
2 cups packed light brown sugar
2½ cups warm strong tea, strained
1 egg, lightly beaten
6 cups self-rising flour
2 teaspoons ground apple pie spice
vegetable oil, for greasing
1 tablespoon honey, to glaze

1 Put the golden raisins, dried currants, raisins and sugar in a bowl. Pour in the tea and stir well. Cover with a clean dish towel and leave overnight.
2 Preheat the oven to 325°F.
3 Grease and line with waxed paper two 9 × 5 × 2¾ inch loaf pans. Grease the lining paper.
4 Stir the beaten egg well into the fruit and sugar mixture. Sift together the flour and spice, then stir into the mixture until thoroughly combined.
5 Divide the mixture equally between the pans. Smooth each surface.

6 Bake the loaves in the oven for 1½ hours, then lower the heat to 275°F and bake for a further 1½ hours, until a warmed fine skewer inserted into the loaves comes out clean.
7 Let the loaves stand for a few minutes until cool enough to handle, then invert them on a wire rack. Turn the loaves the right way up, before glazing the tops with honey.
8 Put the honey in a small saucepan and heat very gently. Brush the tops of the warm loaves, to glaze. Leave until completely cold.

Irish soda bread

Makes 24 slices

4 cups all-purpose flour
1 teaspoon baking soda
1 teaspoon salt
3 tablespoons diced butter or shortening
1¼–1½ cups plain buttermilk
all-purpose flour, for dusting

1 Preheat the oven to 400°F. Sift a thin dusting of flour over a baking sheet.
2 Sift the flour, soda and salt into a bowl, then cut in the butter. Make a well in the center and pour in 1¼ cups buttermilk. Mix quickly to a soft dough with a fork, adding more buttermilk if necessary.
3 With floured hands, gather the dough together, transfer it to a floured surface and knead lightly and briefly until smooth. Shape the dough into a round, about 7 inches in diameter, then place on the prepared baking sheet.
4 Score the round in quarters. Bake the bread in the top of the oven for about 30 minutes, until golden brown and the underside sounds hollow when tapped.
5 Transfer the bread to a wire rack, cover with a clean dish towel and let cool. To serve, break apart into wedges, then slice. Serve warm with butter, and cheese if liked.

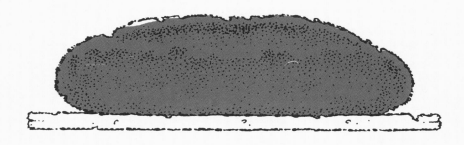

Sweet bun ring

Makes 10 buns

⅔ cup lukewarm water
2 tablespoons superfine sugar
1½ teaspoons active dry yeast
3 cups all-purpose flour
½ teaspoon salt
2 tablespoons margarine or butter
finely grated rind of ½ small lemon
½ cup cold milk
¼ teaspoon vanilla
vegetable oil, for greasing
GLAZE
2 tablespoons sugar
2 tablespoons water
1–2 teaspoons sesame seeds, to decorate

1 Put the water in a small bowl. Stir in 1 teaspoon of the sugar and sprinkle the active dry yeast on the top. Mix well. Set aside in a warm place for 15–20 minutes until the mixture becomes frothy.

2 Sift the flour and salt into a warmed large bowl. Cut in the margarine and rub it in until the mixture resembles bread crumbs. Stir in the lemon rind with the remaining sugar.

3 Make a well in the center of the mixture and pour in the yeast mixture with the milk and vanilla. Using a wooden spoon, mix to a soft dough. Place on a well-floured surface and knead for about 10 minutes, until the dough is smooth and elastic.

4 Oil a large baking sheet. Divide the dough into 10 equal-size pieces and shape into balls. Place in a ring on the prepared baking sheet, so that they just touch one another.

5 Cover with oiled plastic wrap and leave to rise in a warm place for about 1¼ hours, or until doubled in bulk.

6 Preheat the oven to 450°F. Make the glaze: Put the sugar and water in a small saucepan and bring to a boil. Remove from the heat.

7 Uncover the bun ring and bake in the oven for 15–20 minutes until risen and browned. Using a spatula, carefully loosen the buns without breaking the ring and transfer to a wire rack.

8 Brush the buns with the glaze, while they are still warm, then sprinkle with the sesame seeds. Let cool, then transfer the ring to a large platter before serving the buns.

Individual cottage loaves

Makes 8

⅞ cup lukewarm water
1 teaspoon sugar
1½ teaspoons active dry yeast
4 cups all-purpose flour
1 teaspoon salt
½ cup warm milk
1 medium egg, beaten, to glaze
oil and flour, for baking sheet

1 Put water in a small bowl. Stir in the sugar and sprinkle the active dry yeast on top. Mix well. Set aside in a warm place for 15–20 minutes until the mixture becomes frothy.

2 Sift the flour and salt into a warmed large bowl. Make a well in the center and pour in the yeast mixture, with warm milk. Using a round-bladed knife, mix all the ingredients into a soft dough, adding a little extra warm water if necessary. Finish the mixing with your hands.

3 Knead the dough on a floured board for 5–10 minutes until it is smooth and not sticky. Return the dough to the large bowl and cut a cross on the top.

4 Cover the dough with a damp dish towel or greased plastic wrap and leave in a warm place for about 1 hour, or until it has doubled in bulk.

5 Preheat the oven to 400°F. Brush a large baking sheet with oil and dust it with flour.

6 Knead the dough again for 2–3 minutes. Divide the dough in 8 pieces, then divide each piece into 2 rounds, one large and one small. Place a small round on top of each large one to make loaves. Push a clean finger or oiled spoon handle through both, making sure a hollow remains.

7 Place the shaped loaves on the prepared baking sheet and cover them loosely with a damp dish towel or greased plastic wrap. Leave them in a warm place for 10–20 minutes, until they have risen by about one-third.

8 Brush the loaves with beaten egg and bake for about 20 minutes or until the loaves are golden and sound hollow when their undersides are tapped. Cool on wire racks.

Quick brown bread

Makes 1 loaf

4 cups Graham flour
2 teaspoons cream of tartar
1 teaspoon baking soda
1 teaspoon salt
2 tablespoons butter
⅔ cup milk
milk for glazing
cracked wheat (optional)
oil and flour for preparing pan

1 Preheat the oven to 400°F. Grease and flour a deep 8 inch round cake pan, and shake out the excess flour.
2 Sift the flour with the cream of tartar, soda and salt into a large bowl. Stir the bran left in the sifter into the flour mixture. Rub in the butter with your fingertips.
3 Make up the milk to 1 cup with water and pour onto the flour. Using a slim spatula, mix to a soft dough.
4 Place the dough on a lightly floured work surface and knead the dough vigorously for approximately 2–3 minutes.
5 Form the dough into a ball and place it in the prepared pan. Press out the dough to fit the pan and brush the top with milk. Sprinkle with cracked wheat if liked.
6 Bake the bread for 45 minutes. Remove the loaf from the pan, turn it upside down, replace it in the pan and bake for a further 20 minutes, or until done. Leave it to cool on a wire rack before serving.

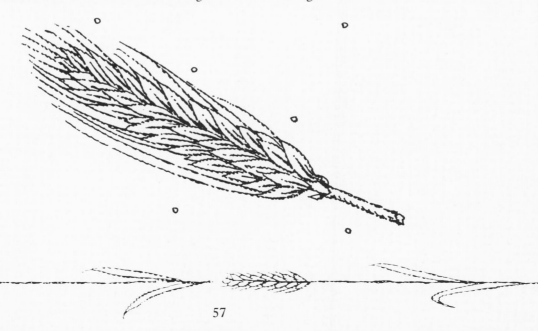

Rich corn bread

Makes one 8 inch square loaf

1 cup cornmeal
1 cup self-rising flour
1 teaspoon baking soda
¼ cup superfine sugar
2 large eggs
⅔ cup milk
¼ cup butter, melted

1 Grease an 8 inch square cake pan. Preheat the oven to 400°F.
2 Put the cornmeal in a large mixing bowl and sift the self-rising flour and the soda on top. Add the sugar and mix together.
3 Beat the eggs with the milk and gradually stir into the flour mixture to make a smooth batter; finally add the melted butter and mix again.
4 Pour the batter into the prepared pan, leveling the surface. Bake for about 25 minutes, until risen and golden brown. Cool the corn bread in the pan, then cut in squares before serving.

Flowerpot loaf

Makes 8–10 slices

1 cup lukewarm water
1 teaspoon sugar
1 teaspoon active dry yeast
1½ cups all-purpose or bread flour
1½ cups Graham flour
1 teaspoon salt
1 tablespoon diced shortening
1 tablespoon bulgur
milk for glazing
vegetable oil, for greasing

1 You require a clean, unused earthenware flowerpot, measuring 5½ inches across the top and 5 inches tall. To season, brush the inside of the pot very thoroughly with oil, then place the empty pot in a preheated 400°F oven for 15 minutes. Allow the pot to cool completely before using.

2 Put the water in a small bowl. Stir in the sugar and sprinkle the active dry yeast on the top. Mix well. Set aside in a warm place for 15–20 minutes until the mixture becomes frothy.

3 Mix the flours together in a large bowl with the salt. Rub in the shortening then make a well in the center. Pour in the yeast mixture and mix to a firm dough.

4 Put the dough on a floured surface and knead for 10 minutes, or until it is smooth and elastic, then shape it into a round to fit in the flowerpot.

5 Brush the inside of the seasoned pot very thoroughly with oil, then sprinkle in 2 teaspoons bulgur. Place the dough in the prepared pot, pressing it down well. Cover with oiled plastic wrap and leave in a warm place for about 1¼ hours, or until the dough has risen just above the top of the flowerpot.

6 About 20 minutes before the dough is risen, preheat the oven to 450°F.

7 Uncover the dough and brush the top with milk. Sprinkle over the remaining bulgur and press it down lightly. Bake loaf in the oven for 40–45 minutes, until the top of the loaf is browned and crusty.

8 Cool the loaf for 2–3 minutes, then run a slim spatula around the side to loosen it. Take the loaf out of the pot, then place the right way up on a wire rack and let cool completely before cutting into slices.

Country loaf

Makes 16–18 slices

1 cup lukewarm water
1 teaspoon sugar
1 package (¼ oz) active dry yeast
4 cups whole grain flour
1 teaspoon salt
extra whole grain flour, for dusting
vegetable oil, for greasing
butter, to serve

1 Brush a 9 × 5 × 2¾ inch loaf pan with oil then set aside in a warm place.

2 Put the water in a small bowl. Stir in the sugar and sprinkle the active dry yeast on the top. Mix well. Set aside in a warm place for 15–20 minutes until the mixture becomes frothy.

3 Put the flour in a warmed large bowl with the salt. Make a well in the center, then pour in the yeast mixture. Using a wooden spoon and then your hands mix to a soft dough, adding more lukewarm water if the consistency of the dough is too stiff.

4 Put the dough onto a lightly floured surface and knead briefly until no longer sticky. Shape the dough into an oblong, then press it out with the heel of your hand until slightly longer and three times wider than the base of the pan.

5 Arrange dough so that the short ends face you. Fold the top third over the center section, then bring the bottom third over the 2 layers. Turn the dough over, so the seam is underneath and tuck the ends under. Place the dough in the prepared pan, pressing it well into the corners to give a good shape.

6 Brush the top lightly with water, then sprinkle with flour. Cover with oiled plastic wrap, or place in a large oiled plastic bag and leave to rise in a warm place for 30 minutes, until the dough reaches the top of the pan.

7 About 20 minutes before the dough is ready, preheat the oven to 400°F.

8 Uncover loaf and bake in the oven for 40 minutes. Remove from the oven and run a slim spatula around the side, then take the loaf out of the pan.

9 Return loaf, upside down, to the oven for a further 5–10 minutes to crisp the base and sides. To test if the loaf is cooked, rap the base with your knuckles – it should sound hollow. Cool completely on a wire rack before cutting. Slice the loaf thickly and serve with butter.

Olive corn bread

Makes 1 large loaf

1¼ cups lukewarm water
½ teaspoon sugar
2 teaspoons active dry yeast
2 teaspoons sea salt
4 cups all-purpose flour
2 cups fine cornmeal plus extra for dusting
½ cup chopped pitted ripe olives
oil for greasing

1 Put half the water in a small bowl. Stir in the sugar and sprinkle the active dry yeast on the top. Mix well. Set aside in a warm place for 15–20 minutes until the mixture becomes frothy. Dissolve the sea salt in the remaining lukewarm water.

2 Mix the flour and cornmeal in a large warmed bowl. Make a well in the center and pour in the yeast mixture and the salt water and stir gradually into the dry ingredients. Add the chopped olives and continue working with a wooden spoon.

3 When the dough becomes too stiff and sticky to work, place it on a board dusted with cornmeal and knead for 15 minutes or until the dough is smooth and pliable.

4 Shape the dough into a ball, oil it lightly and place it in a 9 × 5 × 2¾ inch loaf pan, filling it about three fourths full. Cover and leave in a warm place until doubled in bulk.

5 Meanwhile, preheat the oven to 350°F. When the bread has risen, bake for 45 minutes or until it sounds hollow when removed from the pan and tapped on the bottom. Let cool on a wire rack before serving.

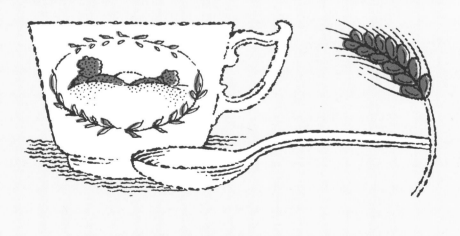

Traditional tea~cakes

Makes 12

4 teaspoons compressed yeast
2 tablespoons superfine sugar
¼ cup half-and-half, plus a little extra
1 tablespoon warm water
2 cups all-purpose flour plus a little extra for dusting
pinch of salt
½ cup butter
oil for greasing
1 teaspoon caraway seeds
butter or whipped cream, to serve

1 Cream the yeast with 1 tablespoon sugar in a small bowl. Mix in the half-and-half and warm water. Set aside for 10 minutes.
2 Sift the flour and salt into a large bowl. Rub in the butter with your fingertips until the mixture resembles fine bread crumbs. Make a well and add the yeast mixture to the center.
3 Mix well, first with a wooden spoon, then by hand, to make a soft dough. Add 1 tablespoon extra half-and-half if needed. Knead the dough well in the bowl until it is smooth and elastic.
4 Dust a baking sheet lightly with

flour. Shape the dough to 12 equal-size balls and place them 3 inches apart on the baking sheet. Flatten the tops slightly and place the sheet in a large, oiled, plastic bag.
5 Leave the tea-cakes in a warm place for 40 minutes or until they are puffy. Meanwhile preheat the oven to 375°F.
6 Brush the tops of the risen cakes with half-and-half and sprinkle with the caraway seeds and remaining sugar. Bake the cakes for 18 minutes, or until they are a light fawn color.
7 Serve the tea-cakes warm, split and filled with butter or whipped cream.

Old-fashioned yeast-raised muffins

Makes 16

1¼ cups milk, lukewarm
1 teaspoon superfine sugar
2 teaspoons active dry yeast
4 cups bread flour
1 teaspoon salt
1 large egg, beaten
2 tablespoons melted butter, plus extra for greasing
butter, to serve

1 Place half the milk in a small bowl. Stir in the sugar, sprinkle the dry yeast over the top and mix well. Then set aside in a warm place for 15–20 minutes until the mixture becomes frothy.

2 In a bowl, sift together the flour and salt, then stir in the yeast mixture, the remaining milk, egg and melted butter. Beat until the mixture is frothy. Cover the bowl and set aside in a warm place for 45 minutes, until the batter has doubled in bulk.

3 Gently heat a griddle or heavy skillet. Check to see if it is hot enough by sprinkling flour over it. The flour should turn brown in 2–3 minutes. Dust the flour off and grease the griddle lightly. Grease 3 inch metal biscuit cutters.

4 Lightly flour your hands and divide the mixture in 16 pieces. Shape the pieces in 3 inch rounds. Press the dough into the metal cutters and cook, in batches, on one side for 5–6 minutes. Remove the cutters, flip the muffins over with a spatula and cook on the other side for 3–4 minutes until evenly brown. Transfer to a wire rack to cool.

5 Split and toast the muffins and serve hot with butter.

Index